The Body is No More Than a Greening Thing

poems by

Louisa Muniz

Finishing Line Press
Georgetown, Kentucky

The Body is No More
Than a Greening Thing

Publisher: Leah Huete de Maines
Editor: Christen Kincaid
Cover Art: Photo by Adrien King on Unsplash
Author Photo: Bryan Muniz
Cover Design: Elizabeth Maines McCleavy

Order online: www.finishinglinepress.com
also available on amazon.com

Author inquiries and mail orders:
Finishing Line Press
PO Box 1626
Georgetown, Kentucky 40324
USA

Contents

For Frank—
the wind beneath my wings

The Body is No More than a Greening Thing

The body named self, named she, named soft,
    composed of stars & dust & longing,

longs for belonging, longs to know from where it's come,
    forever chasing, forever racing to slake

the burning in its bones. But isn't it pretty?
    Body husk of skin, pressed paper thin,

deer limbed to guard the walls within, it's too much
    of this, never enough of that, forever walking

some kind of straight line, some kind of divine.
    Oh, the muscle, node & nerve of it

    the grand gland & gall of it, fighting its communion of lies,
    it denies what it wants, defies what it needs,

confesses on the caps of its knees in all its beauty & bleed.
    This body of tender lemon & light, this greening thing

of fleeting spring will one day be no more, no more
    than a fleeting sparrow of thing, a holy spirit of broken wing.

Under the Lemon Tree

I am from wood, warm & the wax of dawn.
The ancient world calls to me, *no te olivides de mi.*
Don't forget me thrums in my head.

I've come here to uncoil
from the mouth of stillness
mortgaged to summer shadows.

The body is the wind of lullaby.
The body is the wind of dreams.
I am the body that can't forget.

Where I'm from rosary beads sing
Santa Maria, Madre de Dios.
Prayers are milk-fed to faith.

Abuela lost her nine-month *gemelas.*
She bled from a speechless heart
into the lakebed of longing.

Her song is elegy under *el arbol de limonero.*
Below the tree: pungent air of lemon fruit.

I am the namesake of twins. I answer to
the ghost of endearment: *mija, nena, mamita.*

Born on the last quarter of a waning moon
in a pixilated heart, I am stretched & zoomed.

I am from the tapestry of *The Last Supper*
hung all year on the living room wall.
Si Dios Quiere is a prayer for possibility.

Someday I'll return to stardust
scattered in the stillness of space.

Shadow of Absence

The sun unfurls in halved-apple light.
Docked boats sway in the Raritan Bay.

Hands resting on the railing, you stand
at the marina with your father.

He's returned, yet again, after weeks away.
Say cheese, your sister says & presses
the button on the disposable camera.

He smiles—a Kodak moment,
broad & infectious, mostly to hide
his doe-wide wound: orphaned at seven.

Next to him, you feign a smile, mostly
to hide the ache of absence, chain stitched
to your plaid skirt's pleated pocket.

How do you navigate love & distance?
Your child within plays numb.

You are growing— thick skin
in the shadow of absence
the high tide of loss.

Overhead, the forgiving light
of the sky centers you.

The seagulls circle without
flapping their wings.

Think November, under a lapis moon—
some birds stay, others move away.

Invocation

When all is said   & done
when too much   is too much,

& enough's enough   let me   remember
how prayer softens   the bladed tongue.

Let me remember how to—
forgive   forget   forgo.

In the midst of purple milkweed,
queen of the prairie
bird of paradise   let me

remember   the sound
of a crow's caw   a raven's squawk
in morning's   amber glow.

So little time.   So much to do.

Only yesterday   hasty words
slid from my tongue.   A trigger

sounding an alarm   I could not
remember   to breathe.

Let the wrecked
red wagon point   north.

Truth be told, let me travel
light   under the shadows

under   the spell
of a moonlit sonata.

When I can't remember
what I'm doing here or how

to release the wind-caught sparrow
let me remember   to ponder Rumi—

there are hundreds of ways
to kneel   & kiss the ground.

Chasing Memories

No longer standing, no longer a place to call home,
the apartment house on Bentley Avenue that held
clanging radiators & plastic covered furniture

where outside we hid behind the gnarled-shaped birch
in games of hide-and-seek & like runaways
we chased the fleeting clouds down the streets

of Chamberlain, Convery & Sofield as the birds called
from the eaves & bees burrowed in the old oak tree
as we flapped makeshift wings to run across

the snaking creek past Rustler's Steak House,
Anderson's Grocery & Hattie Mae's who swore
her mama kept a quacking duck in the bathtub,

past my best friend Chrissie's house where savory traces
of pierogi hung mid-air near the neighbor's laundry
strung on thirty foot lines as wind fluttered in shirt sleeves,

flapped in pant legs, billowed ghost-like in bed sheets,
much like the memories I chase of the apartment house
no longer standing, no longer a place once called home.

When God Lived in New Jersey

As a child I believed God lived in New Jersey.

When he grew tired of living with the homeless
he moved under our hickory tree.

The cardinal flanked in tree sap
let me know he was always near.

Today, where I'm from, rain hammers the earth.

Noxious weeds—yellow dock, baneberry,
hemlock—gnaw at my sleep.

I plant marigolds to repel earwigs feeding in the night.
Where I'm from, it would be too clichéd to build a wall.

Words implode, tiny firecrackers
under my skin—

Climate Change   Gun Control
Coronavirus   Border Wall

I'm tempted to become a Venus flytrap
to hold in grief.

In dreams I dodge-ball shadows
after watching the news.

That's a good question indicates
the speaker has no idea how
to answer said question.

That's a good question has the moon
spinning stone, the sea spitting foam.

Resurrection

By then I was learning to will things into being.
By then I was leaning into trees.

When the landscaper wrenched you
from the ground to build a deck in the yard,

the earth gasped, the ground rumbled—
snapped, splintered, split.

The sky spit teeth, geese caught
in the crossfire, screamed.

It won't live, said the landscaper
when I asked him to replant you.

~

After the transplant the moon
sugar-lit on silver shadows.

Your leaves wilted, curled, rolled.
A ruffle of breath remained in your trunk.

Daily, I spoke to you
through the kitchen window.

Evenings, I anointed your limbs
with essence of nard.

I cleansed your trunk
with the locks of my hair.

The neighbors shook their heads,
rolled their eyes & drew the shades.

In time, your hickory branches raised.
In time, earth sang its praise.

Gone Missing

Who are we without the birds & bees,
the turtles & trees?

The world unravels a little more
each time a species goes extinct.

Yet, without warning, God's gone missing.
Could it be: seeking answers for the endangered species?

Could it be: manning a backup plan for the race,
shepherding for iCloud space?

It's that time of year when amber light spills
onto the green growing world.

This is how it is: wherever I go, there I am.
I name God in the magnolia, maple & willow,

some days in the raven, robin, wren.
I've spent a lifetime shouldering the nameless.

I've spent a lifetime floating aimless,
light as air in a helium balloon.

I cry myself a river, surrender to the hymn
of what's gone lost, what's gone missing.

What's missing is kindness. It's kindness
for the beaten heart of the world.

Fever Dream of No Regrets

If we are created in God's image,
shaped in tall shadows of longing

like the Sassafras & Oak
as fleeting as the glistening

morning dew—then why
can't we be as candescent

as summer peaches
painted in a still life?

~

When they ask you
what it was like, tell them—

each morning you climbed
through April's window

honeysuckled in butter-lit sun
& not once were you bridled

by the ambling elephant
of large regrets.

Spirit Animal

Somehow, wolf, all that pacing in the wilderness
beyond the meadow finally has my attention.

No longer can I ignore the stalking back & forth.
Why won't you let up? Reveal yourself.

In the world between worlds the veil is thinnest now
where spirit & body commingle.

Although the icy thigh of winter nears
I've kept you small in the seed of my belly.

I am prepared to shape-change, follow
sacred instincts as the sky hails the sea.

I am prepared to recast my shadows
in fire rings around the moon.

When the sun settles, lead me
to the well between the tall pines.

Here we will balm old scar tissue
gather up lost bones hidden underworld.

Through night wind we will resurrect our heart
back to our heart, sing our voice back to song.

Moonstruck & soul-footed
in animal loveliness we will sprint

across muddy waters, where the river
beneath the river softens.

Self-Portrait as Wolf

For weeks—
gather bones.
Meander underworld.

Dig for fossils lost.
Roam restless
with yellow-orbed eyes.
Follow the fog.

Hounded, hunted, harassed,
warm-blooded in wilderness.
Tune ears to hear
silence in fertile soil.

Sometimes the earth is firm
beneath the feet. Other times,
it grips, swallows, slips.

Nose in the wind,
footprints in rain,
this soft animal body
powers in dark.

Ravenous beast.
Bloom wild in the belly.
Hock, flank, fangs—
howl on all fours, four-squared.

What matters most is tinted
light in a toothless moon.
All memories erase in air.

Track familiar scent.
Stalk the way home.

Ten Days to Contemplate the Moon

1

Out of God's gaping eye
fell the moon—hub of the night sky.

2

Nothing moved the waning moon
more than the stars obsessed
with feeding it more light.

3

Under a moonbeam, the trumpet flowers
sang from their fluted throats.

4

There are things I will never hold:
snow geese, birdsong, moon-dust,
the color of indigo blue.

5

The beauty of love can hurt.
The love of beauty can heal.
Moon-dark air blinks back tears.

6

Shaped by July's shadows of a buck moon,
collected moonlight breaks me whole.

7

I've spent a lifetime studying forgiveness.
Holiness mirrors all things moonlit.

8

An orchid, potted, is a poem.
A moonflower, night-blooming
is morning's glory.

9
When I feed the good wolf I am moonlight
trembling through the quaking aspen.

10
The moonseed I plant breathes clarity.
All buds bloom female.

Maw of Silence

What if things didn't turn out
  the way you planned?

When you know better but only
  sometimes, do you do better?

What if joy lifts you by the palm of its hand
  and climbs its way out of the dream?

Don't ask. See how every living thing
is sprung from the silent maw.

See how every living thing speaks to you
nudging you to listen deeper.

Hear the deep hum coming from the earth.
The dogwood foams blossoms into the tree.

The tulips bow into the muscle of you.
Bend your ear. Hear the language of longing.

The swan in the pond floats straight towards you
nodding & bobbing its head saying,

yes, I see you, I see you too.

Isolation in D Minor

Wet newspapers, dirty laundry
& recyclables pile up for days.

The sun hides under a wet dress.
The ants persevere. Push

breadcrumbs across the floor
to the sound of God's pounding fist

in Mozart's Requiem D Minor.
Droning fridge, barking dog

ticking clock rim the day.
The fortune cookie reads,

the fortune you seek is in another cookie.
Yet, I have been blessed in this life.

Blessed art thou amongst...
Will only the meek inherit...?

The cloudless sky babies itself blue.
When the sun offers her self-care

I clear the weeds, prep the soil,
 soak the bulbs.

Plant the snowflake flower
nose up for late spring bloom.

I Learn to Appreciate Soft Butter on Our Vacation

Being brave in rain is not easy. When it stops
I sit outside the restaurant next to the hospital.
Running back & forth to see you, hooked up

to beeping & buzzing machines, broadens the balloon
in my chest. The waiter sets soft butter packets
on the table. I smile, remember you saying—

if I owned a restaurant I'd never serve hard butter.
It's impossible to spread. My phone reads 11:11,
a sign the universe conspires in my favor. The birds

converge on the breakfast crumbs under the table.
Amy Winehouse aches through the speakers.
Since I've come home my body's been a mess.

I've missed your ginger hair, the way you like to dress.
The lady behind me swoons into her phone,
Anthony, you would just love it here.

The island air contracts in my throat
& collected sunlight ushers the poppies to open,
the lilies to lift. If you were sitting here now,

we'd just surrender to being caught in the quiet
cleaving to all we've become—shadows sun-polished
on a porch, birdsong, butter soft light.

On Hearing My Apology to the Birds

Outside the kitchen window, birds rasp & wing-clap
at the empty feeder I've been too busy to refill.

So much complaining, I say to no one
as I marinate the rib eye, saute the zucchini

& steam the string beans. I'm cooking two meals.
One for my husband, the other for my son.

I, too, complain— how quickly time moves
like sand raining through my hands.

I, too, am hungry—to quell this unnamed longing,
this hollow stew of stunted blooms.

Baking chicken takes too long, I tell myself.
I check the center. Cut near the bone.

Still pink. Reminds me of all the undone
I've yet to get done. Nyjer, millet, suet—

is that what they forage for? *I'm sorry*, I whisper
to the birds. I turn down Bocelli's, *Because We Believe*

on the radio. I grab the non-slip oven mitt. Slide out
the drumsticks & thighs. *It's okay, I can wait,*

my husband quips back from the family room.
I smile at the buttered greens. Breathe into the moment.

I scribble *buy birdseed* on my to-do list.
I knead my hunger till it slumbers in my hands.

Next time, the birds will wing-clap in gratitude.
Next time I cook, I will wash the rice in grace.

Empty Nest

All summer long the mourning dove sits
in a shaded crook of the hickory tree.

She nests in a hard-to-spot space
and waits for her forthcoming squabs.

Stock-still, she sits, morning, noon & night.

Our eyes lock as I water the begonia plant
hanging on the tree's branch.

The wind slows, then stirs to shape
& shift the air around us.

All summer long I waited for things to fall in place.
Before the surgery, the doctor asked,

would you like a picture of the kidney
you'll be donating to your husband?

Days later, at home, I prop the picture
on my desk next to the window.

Beyond the window, sunlight leaks
like lemonade into the empty nest.

The song of the mourning dove can be heard.
The shadow of the mourning dove cannot be seen.

Some things resound long enough to be missed.

Musings of a Fool

My body mellows as the bee population
disappears at an alarming rate. The wind squalls,
closes in on me. The invasive lantern fly mills
around the tomato plant growing out of a crack
in the cement. I've lived in pursuit of doing
the right thing. It's like this: as a small boy
you giddy-upped on a spring-coiled horse,
rocked a Stetson hat & cowboy boots & gnashed
your teeth like a wild thing. You once pleaded,
don't ever give up on me. Give up on you?
I've saved your stick figure drawings, a lock
of your first haircut & bronzed your Stride Rite shoes.
Give up on you? I would as soon give up on the long
shadows of the oak or the wind serenading the willow.
Even now as twilight splinters through the dark &
the ruby-winged lantern bugs thrive, I'm a fool
for God's handiwork. Am I a fool for believing
I did the best I could? It's not the living, but more
the forgiving as I draw near the waistcoat of my years.

Fear Sleeps in a Lavender Pillowslip

Out of the corner of my eye
      I watch her watching me.

When the moon is full in June
      she crawls into my lap.

I lull her to sleep. Drape her
in a faux fur throw.

I Hail Mary for her. Full of grace
      she shrinks to the size of a wrist.

I turn on the night-light. Spray
      the pillowslip in lavender.

Her could've, would've, should'ves fade away.
      ~

I wake to morning glories unfurling pink silk.
      The almost summer sun is full-blown

in the green & growing of June.
      I search everywhere. She's ghosted.

Soon she'll return fretting to be held
hanging on the hairs of my head.

Mute as the Mouths of Trees

Winter's sky is bleached in silence.
Outside a red bird perches

on the icy fingertip of a branch.
Somewhere beyond the somber sky

lies heaven—
        mute as the mouths of trees.

Fifteen years you've been gone.
I still search for signs—

the smell of your perfume, a random coin,
a lockbox of breeze in the room.

The year you left I chased your shadow
in the wilderness of dreams.

I've yet—
        to friend uncertainty.

Listen how the wind shapes your name
in the veins of the leaves.

Stay, stay, I whisper to the red bird.
Make your nest this way.

Conjure

There is the dream & there is the dress.
You're twenty-five & I'm six again.

You wear your springy black hair in iconic style
like the movie stars of the forties.

In pink light, you wear a fitted little black dress,
the taffeta one with the floral brocade.

The one Father forbade you to wear.
The one he slashed with the kitchen scissors

you kept in the Bustelo coffee can
beside the stick matches to light the stove

in our Chamberlain Street apartment.
I still taste the smoke & dust trailing his shadow.

String of Hearts. String of Pearls. Peace Lily. Bamboo.
Your house plants: a salve to salvage you.

Listen, the cardinal is calling out back again,
a pure repetitive whistling sound,

loud & florid, it flaps its matador wings,
flies back & forth from the hickory tree.

Is it you?

I've spent my life, wind-caught & wheel spun.
But look what I conjure up to keep you alive—

a dream, a dress, a bird, a plant
alongside a bowl of longing

to carry the loose threads
I tie up in empty hands.

Elegy for a Mother's Daughter
—for Ev

We sip chamomile tea in robin's-egg-blue cups
at my sister-in-law's house.

In the background Etta James croons: *my heart
was wrapped in clover* and *here we are in heaven.*

My eyes fix on her face as we reminisce and she says,
Laura would be turning forty but in my dream, she's three.

*I hold her tight. Remember that time in the kitchen she watched
her reflection in the oven glass door? How she danced and twirled.*

Just seven, maybe she was called back to dance with the stars.

Once again, I quiet against the balm of sorrow.
Once again, I quiet against the ice of silence.

I think of the Thwaite, nicknamed the Doomsday Glacier,
melting at an alarming rate and how it supports
the massive Antarctic ice sheet and how in the dark,

it must seem as buoyant and glistening as a star,
and how it must be as majestic and faceless as God.

Things We'll Never Hold

And what did I know
of the world at twenty-six,

the year I was suppose to
give birth in the spring,

the year Mount St. Helens erupted,
the year John Lennon was shot?

Maybe my longing
should have been less.

Maybe my body
should have done more.

~

All season long a stilled lullaby
beats between barren ribs.

The geese bleed
into the sunset.

Should I believe,
what will be, will be?

~

Near Puget Sound a mother orca
pushes her dead calf around

the waters for seventeen days
and one thousand miles.

She struggles to keep her baby afloat
before letting go.

How long do we carry
the things we'll never hold?

How long do we carry the stories
that need to be told?

Elegy for a Butterfly

—for Dylan Hockley, six year old victim of the Sandy Hook
Elementary School shooting

Once   I believed
grace like rain falls on everyone.

Beyond the window a Holly Blue flits
from bergamot to forget-me-not.

I dream it's hard to breathe
on ocean floor.

Monarch, Mourning Cloak,
Clouded Yellow—

What's in a name?
A boy, with eyes of cornflower blue

loved plain spaghetti
& jumping on trampolines

once told his mom
                    I am a beautiful butterfly.

After rain the gun-metal sky
seeps   emptiness.

Forget-me-nots upended
like torn wings   fall to earth.

I Ask God to Turn Up the Volume Upon Hearing the News of Pittsburgh

God, why have you grown so silent?

In prayer I bloodlet sadness
splintered thin on wooden floors.

Time stands still. Demons root
in the marrow of living.

To blow-soften daily news I wear
rose-colored glasses & cordless ear plugs.

Help me understand. Lift me
from darkness to alpenglow.

Turn up the volume. Say
what you need to say.

The quiet nails my throat.
Even the trees are growing ears

in the netted veins of their leaves.
Daily, I sweeten bread in blessings.

On good days I find you in the bolt
of cherry blossoms riotous blooms,

in the swelling of apricot skies &
the plaiting patterns of sunlit branches.

When they say,
            It's a terrible day for this country,

Don't you think we love hard enough?

After Watching World News

Some days my body carries less of the holy
more of the grief it can't help but hold.

On days I don't know how to take
one more of the world's sorrows

I make of myself a light, needle-colored
under a moon threaded in funeral cloth.

When my fifteen year old granddaughter tells me,
I'm working on becoming a kinder, better person,

last night's news lingers in my head: hostages,
bodies, guns, the thistle & thrum of all we've done.

Why do we hold back our good will?
The one thing we could give of ourselves.

Who knew despair could be a palpable thing?
Yet, the heart allows both light & dark to enter it

as it commits & contracts to the ocean of its wants.
On any given bankrupt morning I might finally stop asking,

where's my stuff to the universe.
Do I really think I'm owed something?

But, if it's still a thing, I'm in the marketplace for gratitude.
Isn't the enough I have, more than enough?

As for hope, I position it mid-height on my tongue,
mid-day in my body, mid-prayer in my burning hands.

ACKNOWLEDGMENTS

I would like to extend my gratitude to the editors and publications that first published these poems (sometimes in earlier versions):

Anti-Heroin Chic: "Under the Lemon Tree"
The Blue Nib: "Chasing Memories;" "Fever Dream of No Regrets"
Claw & Blossom: "Elegy for a Mother's Daughter"
The Fantasy Magazine: "Self-Portrait as Wolf"
Gyroscope: "Conjure"
Jabberwock Review: "On Hearing My Apology to the Birds"
Jelly Bucket: "Elegy for a Butterfly" (Pushcart Prize nomination); "Ten Days to Contemplate the Moon"
Lothlorien Poetry Journal: "Gone Missing;" "Invocation"
The Lumiere Review: "Spirit Animal"
ONE ART: "Empty Nest;" "After Watching World News"
The Rising Phoenix Review: "When God Lived in New Jersey" (Best of the Net Nomination); "Things We'll Never Hold"
Shark Reef: "I Learn to Appreciate Soft Butter on Our Vacation" (Best of the Net nomination)
Sheila-Na-Gig: "I Ask God to Turn Up the Volume Upon Hearing the News of Pittsburgh;" Shadow of Absence"
SWWIM: "The Body is No More Than a Greening Thing"
Thimble Literary Magazine: "Musings of a Fool"
Tiny Seed Journal: "Resurrection"
Trouvaille Review: "Maw of Silence"
Writing In A Women's Voice: "Fear Sleeps in a Lavender Pillowslip;" "Mute as the Mouth of Trees;" "Isolation in D Minor" (Winner of the Moon Prize)

Louisa Muniz was born and raised in Perth Amboy, NJ. The Body is No More Than a Greening Thing is her second chapbook collection. Her poems have been nominated for Best of the Net and a Pushcart Prize and have appeared in numerous anthologies, blogs and literary journals including *SWWIM, Sheila-Na-Gig, One Art* and *PANK Magazine*, among others. She won the *Sheila-Na-Gig* Prize in 2019 and the Writing in a Woman's Voice prize in 2022. She has other work forthcoming in publications. Her debut chapbook, *After Heavy Rains*, published by Finishing Line Press, was released in December, 2020. She is a former K-4 literacy coach, reading specialist and National Board Certified Teacher who traveled to China to participate in an exchange of educational ideas and strategies. Louisa holds an MA from Kean University in Curriculum and Instruction. She currently lives in Sayreville, N.J. with her husband, Frank.